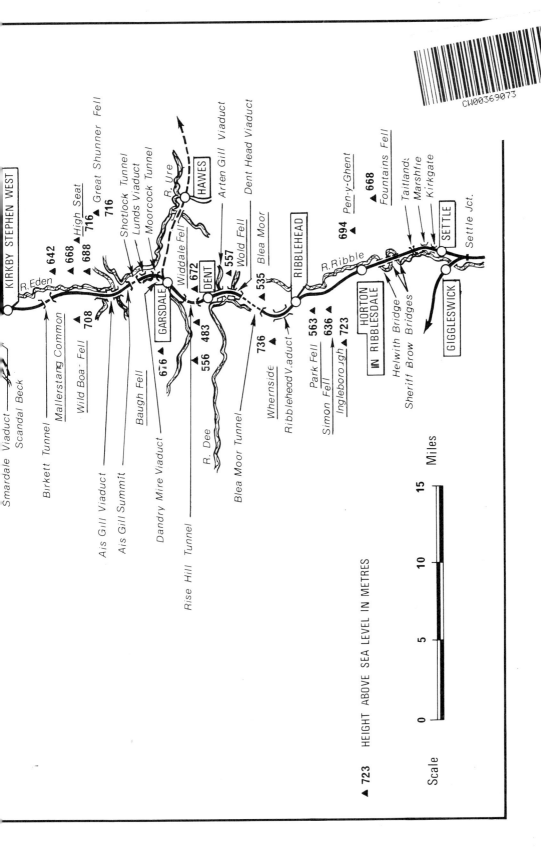

KIRKBY STEPHEN WEST

R.Eden

Smardale Viaduct
Scandal Beck

Birkett Tunnel
Mallerstang Common

▲ 642
▲ 668 ▲High Seat
▲ 688 ▲716 Great Shunner Fell
716

Wild Boa - Fell
▲ 708

Ais Gill Viaduct
Ais Gill Summit
Baugh Fell

Shotlock Tunnel
Lunds Viaduct
Moorcock Tunnel

R. Ure

HAWES

Arten Gill Viaduct
Dent Head Viaduct

GARSDALE

Dandry Mire Viaduct

Widdale Fell

▲ 676 ▲
556 ▲ 483 ▲

DENT
▲ 672

557
▲ Wold Fell
Blea Moor

535 ▲

Pen-y-Ghent
694
▲
▲ 668
Fountains Fell

Rise Hill Tunnel

R. Dee

Blea Moor Tunnel

Whernside
736 ▲

Ribblehead V.aduct

RIBBLEHEAD

R.Ribble

Park Fell 563 ▲
636 ▲
Simon Fell
Ingleborough ▲ 723

HORTON
IN RIBBLESDALE

Helwith Bridge
Sheriff Brow Bridges

Taitlandะ
Marshtie
Kirkgate

SETTLE

Settle Jct.

GIGGLESWICK

Miles

▲ 723   HEIGHT ABOVE SEA LEVEL IN METRES

Scale

0   5   10   15

ON THE SETTLE & CARLISLE ROUTE

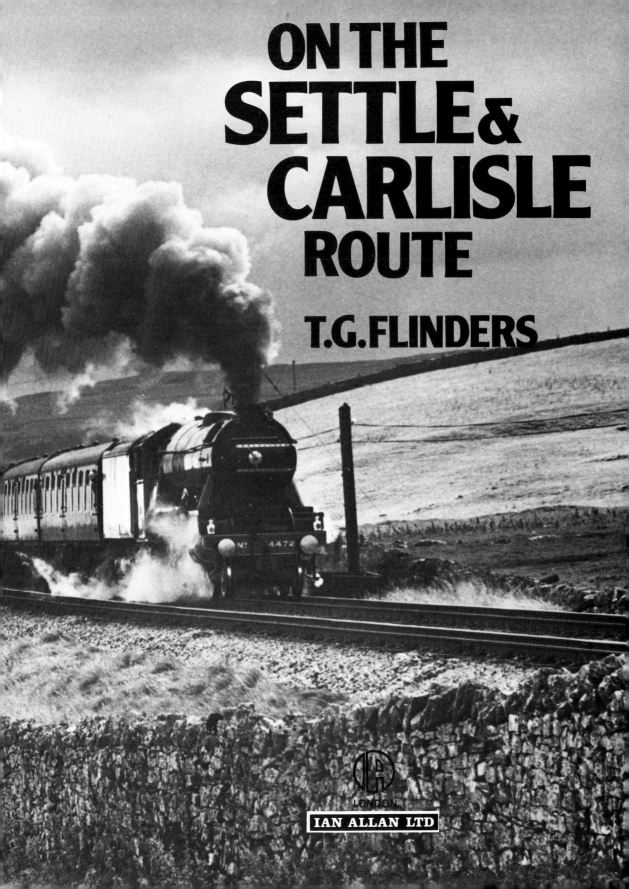

ON THE
SETTLE &
CARLISLE
ROUTE

T.G. FLINDERS

LONDON

IAN ALLAN LTD

The beast of Blea Moor

ONE Autumn eve when I was young
    and steam was growing old,
I stood upon a heathered hill
    above the Widdale road.
And higher yet cloud tousled heads
    of mighty Ingleborough,
Scorned with a grey indifference
    my trespass on Blea Moor.
How great appear the works of man
    beside the valley stream.
How small when viewed from off the hill
    becomes the human dream.
As ever higher rise the hills
    the more man seeks to climb
And prove himself the master yet
    of Nature, space and time.

Sovereign I stood upon the heights,
    my thoughts omniscient
But feeling in that awesome place
    still insignificant.
At one with moor and sky and wind:
    free Fancy's wings unfurled.
Was I a speck no more than dust,
    or dreamer of the World?
Wait: for an alien call disturbed
    my transcendent commune.
Borne on the wind across the fell
    came a melodious tune.
Did brave Diana hunt the Chase
    across the Langstrothdale?
Or were the howling Valkyries
    out riding on the gale?

Again the call, as of a horn
    but now another sound;
Of distant hooves of some great beast
    that lordly pawed the ground.
Rising and falling on the breeze,
    yet ever nearer came
And then, outlined against the sky,
    a proudly flying mane.
Onward it came with furious roar;
    raging across Selside,
Once checked its pace, as if the power
    had failed to match the pride.
Then on once more, balance regained,
    storming into full view;
Out on the limestone viaduct,
    sounding a brave halloo.

Slowly each arch around the curve
    showed progress on the way.
The proud mane now stood out ahead
    marking the wind's strong sway.
Past Gunner Fleet and Winterscales
    and into Little Dale;
Below me now, pace quickening,
    snorting the last assail.
The mane tossed briefly at the point
    where Force Gill crossed the ride
And then the beast was lost to sight:
    plunged in the black moorside.
A light came on in Blea Moor box;
    Imagination palled.
Thoughts of hot soup put dreams to flight:
    A lone sheep curfew called.

               T.G.F.

Contents

First published 1981
Reprinted 1989

ISBN 0 7110 1080 3

Published by Ian Allan Ltd, Shepperton, Surrey; and printed by Ian Allan Printing Ltd at their works at Coombelands in Runnymede, England

Preface

This is not a history book and does not claim to be a definitive study of the railway line it portrays. Many of these already exist and the interested enquirer for whom this present volume is a first encounter with the Settle-Carlisle railway could happily engage himself for several years in studying them. If it is not a history it is, perhaps, a love story and as such it can never be complete, for the love (some would call it obsession), continues. Like all good love stories, it contains moments of sadness as well as joy but I have tried to show the atmosphere of the Settle-Carlisle line as it comes over to me. In this respect then the volume is a story of the Dales rather than the line itself and concentrates on what are to me the most interesting sections through which it passes to the exclusion of others of less impact and interest.

The work was planned as essentially a modern record, although it is at the same time a work of nostalgia, for to me nostalgia is a living thing. I can feel nostalgia over the replacement of the lineside telegraph poles, whilst welcoming the new photographic viewpoints which their absence presents. None the less, for many the nostalgia of the S&C must be synonymous with memories of the age of steam and I have been fortunate in securing the assistance of those two eminent photographers Les Nixon and Gavin Morrison to spice my relatively recent cake with some splendid records of steam's final fling. In return I am happy to accord them a small share of my magnificent obsession! If further credit for anything of merit in this volume is to be given then it should go to those who work on, or over, the line in all its moods and for whom the romance of a snow swept platform is sometimes difficult to understand! Thanks also to the workers and tireless negotiators of the Steam Locomotive Operators' Association without whom steam would have remained dead on this and other main lines and whose successful programme of steam in 1978 gave endless pleasure to those who never knew the S&C when the name 'Long Drag' was born in the sweat and wind and aching backs of the footplate.

The searcher for three-quarter front shots may not enjoy this volume. The view from the ballast changes little between Brighton and Thurso and my interest is in showing the line in its environment, a story of greater and more continuing interest than that told by full frontal noses. All noses look alike if one stands close enough but it follows that this is in no way the final photographic record of the Settle-Carlisle railway. There is ample evidence within of how rapidly changes in both the scenery and locomotive power take place. There is always another day. There is always the ideal combination of motive power, of scenery, viewpoint or lighting and there are many pictures in this book which I would wish to take another day, if only . . .

Introduction

The story of the conception and birth of the Settle-Carlisle line has been written, rewritten, analysed and reanalysed many times. Consequently I will confine myself here to the essence of that history which lies in the fact that the line formed the link which gave the Midland Railway Co a direct route to Scotland and thereby made it a competitor with the Great Northern and the London & North Western Railway Cos. The origins of the line go back to the mid-1850s and arose out of the Midland's difficulties in gaining access to Scotland via Tebay and the 'little' North Western line to Ingleton. Work commenced on the line in 1869 and the first passenger trains ran in 1876. Magnificent in both concept and execution it is somewhat surprising to find that in both time and cost the Midland Railway seriously underestimated the difficulties of construction. Nowadays it is considerably easier to gain access to the Dales but anyone who has stayed for even a week in a holiday cottage, tried to repair a slightly damaged stone wall, walked across a waterlogged field or even attempted to walk a few hundred yards in any of the extreme conditions of weather which occur in those northern climes would define the task of building a railway through such terrain as 'impossible'.

It is surely not without significance that, whilst fine modern roads parallel both the East Coast and West Coast main lines and major highway improvements have occurred throughout the country entailing endless improvements to bridges and straightening of the rolling English road in the sleepiest of rural areas, a car journey from Settle to Carlisle (other than by recourse to the M6) remains a test for the patience, endurance and skill of the driver and the reliability and flexibility of the vehicle. Communication in the Dales country was along the dale. Sheep and hardy souls may go by the short way from one Dale to another but sane men went the long road and indeed to seek to take the short cut, for instance the 'coal road' over Widdale from Dent Head to Garsdale can be impossible because of snow for weeks at a time.

This was the country through which the Midland drove its magnificent way. Had a minor railway meandering along the valley bottoms, bent on nothing more important than the collection of a few milk churns been all that was required, then major engineering works would have been unnecessary but this was to be a main line, and this, it was decided, meant limiting the maximum ruling gradient to 1 in 100. To achieve this entailed substantial engineering works over the whole of the route, climbing in one instance from Settle to Ais Gill, in the other from Carlisle to Ais Gill and scorning both the tempting ease of the floor of the Eden Valley in the northern section and the lowest contours of the Ribble Valley in the south. Always and everywhere, from both north and south, the line is intent on achieving the 1,000ft contour to pass through the true 'mountain' section via Blea Moor and the side of the valleys of the Dee at Dent Dale and the Clough by Garsdale. It is this struggle against the restraints imposed by the topography of the Dales which makes the Settle-Carlisle unique. Not only was the struggle, indeed it still *is*, against the often appalling weather conditions but it was against the resistance of the mountains to be crossed. Even today the elements combine with the geology of the area to seek to restore the landscape to its primeval state and ultimately, in the fullness of time, to level it totally in readiness for the next cycle of earth movements which create new mountains. Ribblehead viaduct is one of the most imposing structures on the line when viewed from beneath its arches but climb the flanks of Whernside or Ingleborough and the insignificance of this mighty structure in relation to the landscape become apparent, and this holds true for many other features on the line. Perhaps if the railway builders of the 19th century had had available to them facilities such as aerial surveys and acoustic techniques for determining the depth and nature of bedrocks they would not have dared to embark upon the exercise. That they dared is a matter of record for the results are there for all to see. But the Settle-Carlisle line is not simply a series of listed structures. In the summer of 1979 there were something like 24 regular freights and six passenger trains during daylight hours and the line is regularly used for diversions for engineering work, when, for instance the WCML is being worked on, or for emergencies such as the ECML Penmanshiel tunnel disaster.

Come with me then and traverse the Midland's Highroad to Scotland, pausing occasionally to mourn what has passed and marvel that such a thing came to be.

Settle Junction to Ribblehead Viaduct

This section encompasses the whole of the Ribble Valley a distance of approximately 13 miles (21km) and sees the transition from relatively verdant pasture and woodland at the commencement of the line at Settle junction to the virtually treeless wastes of Batty Moss. None the less the scenery has a certain common theme in that it is dominated by the massive grey/white crags of the Great Scar limestone both in natural landmarks and the works of man. The line climbs from an approximate elevation of 450ft (140m) OD to something over 1,000ft (305m) OD. Directly Settle viaduct is left behind, the countryside rapidly takes on an impression of grey-green arising from the subtle blending of turf and white limestone. There is little arable farming but an unbroken tradition of sheep grazing stretching back to the time of the original Norse settlers. It is this sheep grazing and latterly cattle grazing, which has contained the continued threat of the return of the prehistoric and medieval forests by 'cutting off at the roots' any sapling unwise enough to attempt the breakthrough. Only in recent years has the Forestry Commission with its wire enclosures and deep ridge ploughing attempted reafforestation and this not with English hardwoods but with that curse of the moors the sitka spruce for which no one to whom one speaks in the Dales seems to have a good word. Spruce plantations notwithstanding, the turf of these areas has remained unbroken throughout most of recorded history.

The lower valley, south of Stainforth, was a relatively easy task for the railway constructors, although the engineering works were always dominated both by the need to reach a level of at least 1,000ft (350m) by Ribblehead and also to be at a reasonable height below Helwith Bridge where the valley narrows into a gorge. This feature forced the contractors into the somewhat drastic measure of diverting the river and the construction of two short but massive viaducts as an alternative to bypassing the gorge completely. In fact the line enters the gorge some 50ft (15m) above river level at an elevation of approximately 650ft (198m) but at Helwith, river and line come together for a brief period, before the line's need to aim for the 1,000ft objective in the mountain section (see part 2) takes it steadily away again and, by the time the desired elevation is reached at Ribblehead, the river is some 100ft (30.5m) below the line.

As the line leaves the short level section in the old glacial lake just north of Helwith Bridge, the skyline comes to be increasingly dominated by the first of the Three Peaks; Pen-y-ghent. It is this mountain rising to 2,273ft (694m) above a relatively level area around 1,000ft (305m) which, above all other, impresses itself upon the rail traveller on their first journey on the Settle-Carlisle line. Shortly thereafter the line runs below the eastern flank of Ingleborough 2,373ft (723m), and, heading towards Whernside 2,419ft (736m), the third of the Three Peaks, reaches the crowning glory, certainly of this section of the line and possibly of the whole enterprise. This is of course the red brick lined, limestone viaduct at Ribblehead. Some 105ft high, it was built between October 1870 and October 1874 and has 24 arches. Many words have been written about this viaduct, for in many ways it epitomises the whole of the spirit of the long drag and many an hour both in steam days and since was spent by railway enthusiasts at its northern end, pensively awaiting the appearance of northbound trains storming towards the first summit in Blea Moor tunnel.

There is a story that British Rail, faced with the massive maintenance costs of this viaduct have prepared a design study to fill in the end arches and replace the centre span with a precast concrete structure. The viaduct is of course a listed structure, but it could be argued that if the alternative to this act of vandalism was the closure of the Settle-Carlisle line itself then the 'modification' would have to be accepted. It would still be a tragedy.

Below: After the Class 50s were transferred from the London Midland Region as the result of the completion of the electrification to Glasgow some were employed for a while working freight over the Settle-Carlisle line. Here No 50.045 waits at the approach to Settle junction on 22 March 1975.

Above: Getting a flying start at the 1 in 100, BR Standard Class 9F 2-10-0 No 92009 speeds past Settle junction with the Widnes-Long Meg sidings empties in the spring of 1967. *L. A. Nixon*

Centre right: In soft late winter sunshine a dmu forming the 14.15 Morecambe-Leeds crosses over from the Giggleswick line at Settle junction in March 1975.

Bottom right: The previous picture shows Settle junction as operating in 1975. As a result of the derailment of all 41 wagons of the St Blazey-Carlisle freight on 1 May 1979 which severely damaged the junction, BR instituted single line working as far as Wennington, using the up line only. In this picture preserved 'Merchant Navy' Pacific No 35028 *Clan Line* has crossed over the junction and taken the former up line bound for Carnforth with the BR organised 'North Yorkshireman' special on 30 May 1979.

Above: The divergence of the older line to Ingleton and the Settle-Carlisle line just beyond Settle junction is clearly seen in this shot of *Clan Line* taking the 'North Yorkshireman' away to Carnforth on a very wet 30 May 1979.

Centre left: On another wet day, not unusual in this part of the world, the 'V2' class 2-6-2 No 4771 is seen between Settle and Settle junction with the up leg of a special on the 27 March 1978.

Bottom left: At last a beautiful spring day, 29 May 1979, and No 45.008 makes a spirited start from Settle with the 09.35 Carlisle-Nottingham. Sugarloaf Hill can be seen in the background and it was in this area, close to the Birkbeck Mansion of Anley that the first sod was cut early in 1870. The road on the left is the A65 trunk road to Kendal whose company the line keeps only until crossing it at Settle viaduct.

Left: With 13 miles of 1 in 100 to go to the mini summit in Blea Moor tunnel Class 9F 2-10-0 No 92125 approaching Settle station on 15 July 1967. *G. W. Morrison*

Below left: As far as most people are concerned it is Settle station which marks the beginning of the Settle-Carlisle railway line. Although its importance has diminished and sidings have been removed in recent years the station itself has remained unchanged. Flower beds and the famous twin arrow sign can still be seen. In the shot No 46.036 rolls to a stand with the 11.50 Glasgow-Nottingham on 19 August 1978.

Right: Settle station's main buildings seen through the imperfect glass of the down platform waiting room in August 1978.

Below: Southbound freight headed by No 40.116 comes into Settle station eagerly awaited by a youthful railway enthusiast on 29 May 1979.

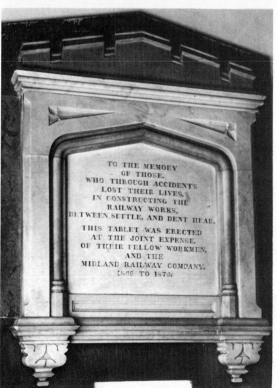

Above & left: Settle church, seen here from the 08.00 St Pancras-Glasgow on 3 April 1976, was less than 30 years old at the time of the construction of the Settle-Carlisle line and contains one of the two commemorative plaques prepared at the joint cost of the contractors and the Midland Railway Co paying tribute to those who sacrificed their lives building the line.

Above right: With traces of snow all around No 40.108 storms up the 1 in 100 just north of the short Stainforth tunnel with the 07.15 Nottingham-Glasgow at 10.17 on 24 March 1979. High hills look down on the line as it keeps company with the Ribble but continues the climb aimed at the ultimate summit of Ais Gill.

Right: No 47.053 is seen climbing above Langcliffe with the 07.15 Nottingham-Glasgow on 29 May 1979. By this point the line is leaving the valley floor well behind in its battle to gain the 1,000ft level.

Above: No 40.084 with the 11.50 Glasgow-Nottingham between Sherriff Brow and Langcliffe, apparently perched on the eastern side of the Ribble Valley on 23 August 1978.

Left: Just north of the previous shot the line negotiates the Ribble's emphatic loop with two stone skew viaducts 300yd apart. At one point the railway took over the former bed of the river. On 29 May 1979, No 47.102 is seen northbound over the more southerly of these two viaducts which is 55ft high.

Above right: A down passenger train crosses the more northerly of the two Sherriff Brow viaducts on 24 August 1978. The viaduct is 25ft high, an apparently minor work, but some idea of the difficulties of constructing the line even in these more southerly sections can be gauged from studying the constantly varying levels around the rock strewn river bed. The shot is taken from B6479, the Settle-Ribblehead road which follows the line of railway and river.

Right: Mundane if arduous duty for 'Britannia' Pacific No 70029 *Shooting Star* passing a '9F' hauled up freight at Stainforth sidings on 18 April 1967. *G. W. Morrison*

Above left: Some slight relief to the railway builders and to generations of struggling firemen was afforded at Helwith Bridge where for a short section of half a mile the line crosses the site of a former glacial lake. In this August 1978 shot, No 47.351 approaches Helwith Bridge with a down van train. Old quarry buildings can be seen in the background. Whilst the relief afforded by the level nature of the ground was welcome, the clay of the area would not afford suitable foundations for bridge building and deep shafts were needed to reach bedrock to support the adjacent bridge carrying the line over the river.

Left: Regular steam working over the full length of the line was considerably reduced with the closure to steam of Leeds Holbeck (55A) with effect from 9 October 1967. Prior to that a regular performer was the, enthusiast cleaned, 'Jubilee' 4-6-0 No 45562 *Alberta* seen here approaching Helwith Bridge with the 13.30 Hunslet-Carlisle on 30 September 1967. Other than the Long Meg sidings-Widnes mineral workings, scheduled steam hauled freight ceased with the closure of Carlisle Kingmoor (12A) with effect from 1 January 1968, the final steam working south being the 13.10 to Skipton headed by No 70045 *Lord Rowallan* on 30 December 1967. *G. W. Morrison*

Above: On a damp and cloudy day in August 1978 No 47.431 approaches Helwith Bridge with the 09.35 Carlisle-Nottingham. The area of level ground left by the drying up of the glacial lake can be clearly seen.

Right: An unidentified 9F says everything about steam on the Settle-Carlisle line as it raises the echoes through Horton-in-Ribblesdale with a down freight on 4 November 1967. *L. A. Nixon*

Above: Although the station is closed, Horton-in-Ribblesdale sidings still give some idea of the appearance of the many stations on the line in its heyday. Here No 45.141 with the 07.15 Nottingham-Glasgow is halted for inspection after a trailing object had been reported under one of the carriages. The picture was taken on 1 June 1979.

Below: This view from Horton-in-Ribblesdale station shows No 47.360 approaching with a down freight in June 1979. The right of way crosses the line at the end of the platform.

Above: Despite the pristine Dales Rail station name board and the distraction of the large bird apparently racing the No 47.424 hauled 09.35 Carlisle-Nottingham through Horton it is clear that the station has seen better days. The grass grown areas on the platform mark the site of the flower beds which once rivalled those of Settle.

Below: Stanier Class 5 4-6-0 No 44886 climbs away from Horton-in-Ribblesdale with a Carlisle freight on 27 September 1963. *G. W. Morrison*

Left: BR Standard Class 4 4-6-0 No 75019 from Rose Grove shed departs Horton-in-Ribblesdale with a down ballast train originating from Grassington quarry on 31 May 1968. The locomotive was maintained in immaculate condition by enthusiasts, this being a regular occurrence towards the end of steam. Note how little the two trees have grown since 1963. *G. W. Morrison*

Below: From spring to deepest winter. The trees are down now as No 47.226 climbs away from Horton-in-Ribblesdale with a Tinsley-Carlisle freight on 22 March 1979.

Top right: Old and (relatively) new in partnership. A British Railways Standard Class 9F 2-10-0 is seen double-heading a Stanier Class 8F near Selside with a down permanent way train in the spring of 1966. *L. A. Nixon*

Centre right: Winter has passed but the clouds remain and the scene at Selside is altogether more depressing than the sunny snow shot seen earlier. No 40.015 is seen with the 11.50 Glasgow-Nottingham passing the double row of railway cottages on a wet and dismal 31 May 1979.

Bottom right: Another dismal day just north of the previous shot is considerably enlivened by the presence of steam. No 4498 takes a down steam special across Selside on 21 October 1978. The cloud capped summit of Pen-y-ghent can be seen in the background.

Left: No 4498 continues her spirited climb across Selside by now well above the Ribble which lies between the embankment and Horton Moor in the background. The cars in the lower part of the picture are on the winding, hilly, B6479 which accompanies the line as far as Ribblehead.

Below left: Double-headed Stanier Class 8F 2-8-0s headed by No 48321 struggle across Selside with a Dewsnap (Guide Bridge)-Carlisle concrete sleeper track train on 26 June 1967. *G. W. Morrison*

Right: The Long Drag was bad enough for a locomotive in good order with its train moving. Having been stopped at Selside in November 1967, this '9F' 2-10-0 No 92082 found steam escaping from every possible place rather than assist in the effort of restarting the train. *L. A. Nixon*

Below: An immaculate No 40.100 with an up train north of Pen-y-ghent on 22 August 1978. The threatening clouds on what is ostensibly a summer day are typical of this area and make a sunlit shot in any particular location a rarity even for the dedicated student of the line.

Top left: Bishop Eric Treacy was one of the finest photographers of his or any other generation and no finer tribute can be offered to him than this photograph of a special bearing his name and hauled by No 92220 *Evening Star*. The special is climbing from Selside towards Salt Lake cottages on 30 September 1978.

Centre left: If proof were needed of the rapidly changing weather conditions which can be encountered in the area of the High Fells this photograph provides it. No 4472 on the 'Lord Bishop' down special has just left a patch of sunlight to torment the photographer and his exposure meter.

Bottom left: Unlike less happy lines now plagued by high speed hornets, many rights of way still cross the Settle-Carlisle line. No 40.156 on an up ballast train approaches one such crossing at milepost 246. The crossing's warning notice can be seen in the earlier shot of No 4472 with the 'Lord Bishop'.

Right: The line has now reached the 1,000ft (305m) level and is about to part company with the River Ribble whose valley it has followed from Settle junction. With Pen-y-ghent in the background, beyond the Salt Lake cottages, so called because of the shanty town which once stood here, this shot, taken just south of Ribblehead shows the almost level country at the 1,000 to 1,200ft level. A double-headed down freight led by No 25.234 meets an up freight headed by No 40.036, on 24 August 1978.

Below: No 46.015 heads south from the site of the former Ribblehead station with the 11.50 Glasgow-Nottingham in August 1978. The siding to the Ribblehead quarry is on the left of the picture and the massive hill in the background is the southern flank of Whernside.

Above: No 46115 *Scots Guardsman* with the RCTS 'Last Scot' special approaches Ribblehead station on 13 February 1965. Although the ground in the immediate vicinity is clear of snow the telegraph poles bear mute testimony to the direction of north-west! Note the entrance to Ribblehead quarry on the right. *G. W. Morrison*

Below: No 25.213 approaches the site of Ribblehead station past the spur into Ribblehead quarry in August 1968.

Above: The remains of the snow drift which enveloped Ribblehead station in the blizzards of mid-March 1979, is passed by No 46.047 with the 11.50 Glasgow-Nottingham on 22 March 1979. The line in the foreground is the spur to Ribblehead quarry.

Below: Threatening skies on 22 March 1979, overshadow No 40.079 going north past the 'Station Inn' at Ribblehead. The slope of Park Fell is in the background The moorlands in such conditions can be extremely treacherous as snow clears from some sections leaving deep drifts which sometimes hide precipitous drops or fast flowing streams which undermine and weaken the snow cover such that the unwary tramper can break through into a freezing torrent.

Above: Ribblehead viaduct seen from the east, the size being apparent only in relation to the southbound Class 40 upon it. Within the cleats in the limestone pavements can be found remnants of the medieval forest which browsing sheep have been unable to remove. This picture was taken on 14 September 1976.

Below: Later the same day an unidentified Class 25 heads north against the background of Ingleborough 2,373ft (723m) with a stone train from Ribblehead quarry. The quarry is used as a concentration area for ballast delivered from other quarries by lorry.

Above: Seen from the Ingleton road on 22 August 1978 the size of the viaduct is once again apparent only by comparison with the northbound Class 40 hauled freight upon it.

Below: A day to remember was 11 August 1968, when steam officially ended on British Rail and was not destined to return to the Settle-Carlisle line until 1978, 10 years later. No 70013 *Oliver Cromwell* is seen silhouetted against Ingleborough as it approaches enthusiasts, grouped at the northern end of Ribblehead viaduct. The moors in general and Batty Moss in particular, were more reminiscent of a fair ground than a national park on this particular day and fortunately the clement weather permitted the many ill attired children and other 'once in a lifetime' moor walkers to survive. *Mrs M. Flinders*

Above: That fine photographer and lover of the Settle-Carlisle line, the Right Rev Eric Treacy died at Appleby station on 13 May 1978, whilst awaiting the arrival of a steam special. In his memory BR organised the running of two special steam hauled trains on 30 August 1978. On a day of rapidly changing weather when sunshine and shadows tested photographers' skills to the maximum, fate and skill combine to arrange that both Ribblehead viaduct and Pen-y-ghent are lit at their best as No 4472 *Flying Scotsman*, raises the echoes forging north with the down leg of the 'Lord Bishop' special. *G. W. Morrison*

Below: Only two years after the end of steam and still in original green livery, 'Peak' No 193 leaves the northern end of Ribblehead viaduct with the down 'Thames-Clyde Express' (09.05 St Pancras-Glasgow) on 12 August 1970. The misty flanks of Simon Fell and Ingleborough in the background are typical of this view and I suspect that the romantic memory which many railway enthusiasts claim of the setting or rising sun lighting the viaduct and Ingleborough as a sparkling clean diesel or roaring steam engine heads for Blea Moor is memorable as much by its rarity as by its undoubted beauty.

Ribblehead to Garsdale

The Ribblehead-Garsdale section is real mountain country. In former times there was a considerable amount of local industry in the Dales including textiles and coal mining, but more particularly the quarrying and polishing of limestone (Dent marble) in Dent Dale, making use of water power to drive the machinery. Nowadays the line passes through locations which men visit only for specific short term purposes, usually to tend the sheep or maintain the railway itself.

Thirteen miles (21km) from Settle junction, 1,050ft (320m) attained; the mountains there for the taking, with a small matter of two tunnels totalling something over $1\frac{1}{2}$ miles (2.4km) and a couple of viaducts to resist progress before the relative civilisation of Garsdale (junction for Hawes).

First the final $1\frac{3}{4}$ miles (2.8km) of 1 in 100 past Blea Moor box to the southern portal of the 500ft (152m) deep Blea Moor tunnel, a stifling plunge through to Dent Head and then what is to me the most beautiful and breathtaking $2\frac{1}{2}$ miles of railway in the United Kingdom. Boldly soaring some 200ft (61m) above the infant Dee, which is itself at an elevation of 800ft (244m) passengers have barely two minutes to take in the almost indescribable beauty of Dent Dale. This is a veritable Yorkshire Shangrilah, for Dent Town was first a British village, later in the 10th century settled by Norsemen but largely ignored or undiscovered by the waves of Angles and Danes and escaping the close attention of the Normans whose castle was at Sedburgh. In the 18th century the development of Sedburgh, consequent on the construction of the Kirkby Stephen to Greta Bridge and Askrigg to Kendal turnpikes led to a decline in the status of Dent Town, but thereby protected the valley from 'development'.

From rail level the appearance of the valley can have changed little in the century since the railway came and the Midland confidently perched Dent station four miles (6.5km) from and 700ft (213m) above the town!

A further cool plunge through Rise Hill tunnel at an elevation of over 1,100ft (335m) and the line emerges on to another ledge, this time the southern side of Garsdale some 300ft (91m) above the Clough river, which runs to and fro across the A684, the sometime Askrigg to Kendal turnpike, constructed on the route of an existing road in the latter half of the 18th century.

Garsdale saw the junction with the former Hawes branch, opened in October 1878 and closed in 1959. The station still possesses some life due to its signalbox and the adjacent row of cottages many of which are available as holiday accommodation and are used by die-hard Settle-Carlisle enthusiasts.

The 8.5 miles (13.7km) of this section lies (or flies) always at an elevation of between 1,100 and 1,150ft (335 and 350m). The totally unimaginative traveller who forebore to raise his eyes above the track, could imagine himself on a more 'normal' railway, for the use of the relatively straight sides of the two glacial valleys of Dent Dale and Garsdale meant that, two tunnels and two viaducts notwithstanding, an alignment and gradient profile more than competitive with many so called lowland mainlines was provided.

This is truly a main line through the mountains.

Left: Continuing the story north of Ribblehead viaduct we see No 92220 *Evening Star* on 13 May 1978 storming away towards Blea Moor with the special referred to on page 32.

Above: Slightly north of the previous shot No 4472 *Flying Scotsman* together with the McAlpine preserved private saloons is seen with a special on 15 June 1978.

Right: Despite the removal of some signalboxes, semi-permanent closure of others and wholesale removal of sidings, certain key boxes have retained their importance and will continue to play a major role in the working of the line in this inhospitable area unless, or until, automation takes over. A key reporting box in the mountain section is Blea Moor the interior of which is shown in 1979. *Peter R. Walton*

Above left, left & above: The 'Farewell to Steam' specials of 11 August 1968, involved *Oliver Cromwell* northbound and a southbound return leg pulled by double-headed Stanier Class 5 4-6-0s No 44781 and 44871. These locomotives worked north 'light engine' coupled together on the morning of 11 August and this series of pictures shows them taking water at Blea Moor. In fact this was one of the most isolated signalboxes on the line since there is no road access to it and the box and the associated (now derelict cottages) lie some ¼ mile from the Ingleton/Hawes road.

Right: No 45.037 brings the 07.15 Nottingham-Glasgow through Blea Moor sidings past the water tank on 10 May 1979. The photograph is taken from an elevation of 1,100ft and the 2,373ft peak of Ingleborough can be seen four miles to the south.

Above: Another shot of the light engines for the 'Farewell to Steam' special sees them approaching the aqueduct which takes Force Gill over the railway line. Beyond the arch of the aqueduct can be seen the dark southern portal of Blea Moor tunnel.

Left: A view from above the southern portal of Blea Moor tunnel taken from an elevation of 1,200ft. The massive cutting originally intended as part of the tunnel can be clearly seen. The locomotive is No 47.005 with 7PO8 Bescot-Carlisle freight on 10 May 1978.

Above right: Up 'Thames-Clyde Express' (09.35 Glasgow-St Pancras) leaves the southern portal of the Blea Moor tunnel pulled by 'Peak' No 25 on 12 August 1970. Note the spoil heaps to the right, above the tunnel mouth. This, together with the slight curvature indicated by the coaches disappearing into the tunnel gives some indication of the curvature of the tunnel itself. The tunnel is some 2,629yd long 500ft deep and is provided with three 10ft dia air shafts, the deepest of which (numbered 3) is at the northern end and is some 390ft deep. The 'Thames-Clyde Express' was inaugurated in 1927. It lost its title with the end of the 1974/75 timetable; all through London-Glasgow working ceased with the introduction of the 1977/78 timetable, daytime through services having ceased with the introduction of the May 1976 timetable.

Right: No 40.108 leaves the northern portal of Blea Moor tunnel with the 07.15 Nottingham-Glasgow on 23 March 1979. The signal just forward of the linesman's hut to the left of the tunnel entrance, is a repeater for the distant signal seen in the cutting at the southern end.

Above: No 25.158 leaves Blea Moor tunnel on 21 July 1977. In this picture the encroaching spruce, planted on behalf of the Forestry Commission is beginning to obscure the view. The only remaining virgin moorland is the section enclosed by the BR wall clearly seen like a somewhat twisted halo around the tunnel portal.

Below: On a vile but typical North Yorkshire day on 13 September 1976, No 45.022 brings the 10.45 Glasgow-Nottingham towards the northern portal of Blea Moor tunnel. The gorse, heather and bracken of the original moorland can be seen in the foreground within the British Rail property. Dent Head viaduct can be seen in the top left hand background.

Above: A Class 40 hauled up freight is seen on Dent Head viaduct on 23 March 1979. The viaduct is of blue limestone, some 100ft high and 1,150ft above sea level.

Below: No 4771 crosses Dent Head viaduct with a return special on 27 March 1978. The erosion of the moorland soil covering can clearly be seen in the foreground. In this wild and often cloudy country the difference between winter and summer shots is often only apparent because of the leaves on the trees.

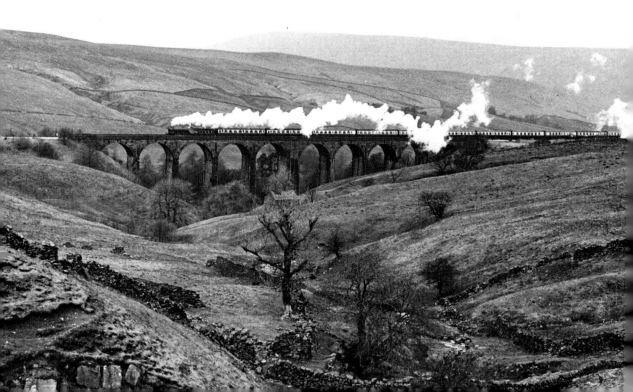

Top left: There is no doubt about the time of year in this shot as No 46.002 brings the 09.35 Carlisle-Nottingham towards Dent Head viaduct on 23 March 1979.

Centre left: Spring. No 25.104 with an engineer's train on Dent Head viaduct is seen from the road which enters the head of the Dale beneath the viaduct and follows the river along the valley floor. 27 May 1979.

Bottom left: Artengill viaduct is, to me, one of the most impressive structures on the line and gives a tremendous impression of height, although it is in fact (at 117ft) only 17ft higher than Dent Head viaduct. The viaduct spans the area where a post glacial stream has cut into the valley side. Here we see No 40.036 with a southbound freight on 25 August 1978. The curve of the line along the side of the valley can clearly be seen and the white building in the centre background is the former station master's house and station at Dent.

Above: Dent Head viaduct appears lower and less impressive than Artengill because it crosses over the road whereas Artengill viaduct is usually seen from the road at Stonehouses some 150ft below its foot. This view shows a Class 40 with a southbound freight viewed from the track which follows Artengill Beck between Dent and Wold Fell and eventually finds its way to the Widdale road to Hawes. Machinery for cutting and polishing Dent marble was housed near this point during most of the 19th century but little trace of the factory can now be found.

Below: A view from above Artengill as No 40.087 crosses with the 07.15 Nottingham-Glasgow on 25 August 1978.

Above left: An unidentified Stanier Class 8F 2-8-0 struggles across Artengill viaduct in a force 8 gale in February 1966. *L. A. Nixon*

Below left: Dent Dale viewed from the station on 23 March 1979. What has the nearer part of continental Europe to offer compared with this?

Above: The blizzards of March 1979, closed the 'coal road' from Dent station to Carodale and considerable drifting took place on certain sections of the line. The author is seen between the snow fences north of Dent station. Despite the poor state of repair of the fences it is clear that snow which could have been blown into the cutting has been deposited on the hillside between the fences. *Stephen Bulman*

Below: Stanier Class 8F No 48077 is seen approaching Dent station with a down freight on 30 April 1967. Artengill viaduct can be seen in the distance behind the signal. *L. A. Nixon*

Above: Sunshine has returned to the Dales and begun to melt the snow, although the effect of the drifts can still be seen in the angle of the signal post on the left hand side of the picture as No 47.416 hurries the 11.20 Nottingham-Glasgow past Dent signalbox and towards the station on 23 March 1979.

Right: The interior of Dent signalbox in 1976. *Peter R. Walton*

Above: More sunshine at Dent on 9 May 1978, as No 45.002 brings the 07.15 Nottingham-Glasgow through the station. Although the station is used in the Dales Rail scheme the station buildings are now used as a school outdoor activity centre.

Centre left: No 40.097 is seen passing Dent signalbox on 9 May 1978. Note the unconventional support to the fence on the left, presumably a partial defence against the weight of drifting snow. The signal post in this shot has not been modified by the snow drift noted in the shot taken in March 1979.

Bottom left: Further confirmation that the Dent signal was not designed to be angled towards the east is provided by this 16 June 1978, shot of No 4472 *Flying Scotsman* leaving the station with a private special.

47

Above left: Bereft of nameplates and looking all of her 32 years Stanier 'Jubilee' class 4-6-0 No 45675 *Hardy* blasts over the summit of the short climb from Risehill to Dent station with an up freight for Stourton in April 1966.   *L. A. Nixon*

Left: Writings on the Settle-Carlisle line mountain section invariably refer to the 'coal road' over Widdale Fell. Notwithstanding the fact that the road is impassable for much of the winter and was to remain a 'green' road until the 1950s the railway builders saw fit to provide it with this massive bridge to cross the cutting approaching the northern end of Dent station. No 40.097 is seen on a Carlisle-Severn Tunnel freight approaching the station from the cutting in May 1978.

Above: This shot of the same bridge from the down platform shows the gradient of this section of the road. Although this photograph of No 4472 *Flying Scotsman* in June 1978, is taken on a beautiful English spring afternoon the steepness of the cutting shows how the track can be blocked by snow and hence the need for the famous snow fences.

Right: Risehill tunnel seen from the cutting north of Dent station. At this point the railway engineers took advantage of the fact that Cowgill Beck had cut back into the southern flank of Dent Dale and this use of the secondary valley materially shortened the length of Risehill tunnel. Cowgill Beck now passes at a considerable depth under the railway embankment and in clement weather it is possible to traverse the stone-lined, cave-like, culvert. No 47.113 is seen approaching Dent on 20 July 1977.

Above: Seen from Doderham Moss to the east of the line is the section which would have been tunnel but for the cutting back of the hillside by Cowgill Beck. No 40.076 leaves the southern portal of Risehill tunnel in May 1978.

Below: As with all Settle-Carlisle scenery the railway quickly begins to disappear as soon as height in gained. This view taken from above the southern portal of Risehill tunnel shows No 40.013 with the 10.20 Nottingham-Glasgow on 15 August 1978. The serried ranks of spruce on the plantation on Doderham Moss to the east of the line can be clearly seen.

Top right: No 25.291 leaves the southern portal of Risehill tunnel in July 1977.

Centre right: The weather did its moorland worst to spoil the photograhic possibilities of the tour on 13 May 1978. In pouring rain with a promise of sun to come, once the train has passed, *Evening Star* is seen from the northern flank of Garsdale leaving Garsdale station towards Risehill tunnel.

Bottom right: More 'weather' at Garsdale as No 40.040 approaches the station at 17.00 on 23 March 1979. The piles of snow have been removed from the approach road to Garsdale cottages. This was as far as snow clearing went and the 'coal road' was, as ever, blocked.

Top left: On a wet and windy 21 October 1978 No 4498 *Sir Nigel Gresley* is seen running into Garsdale to take water.

Centre left: A slight break in the fog allows a quick glimpse of No 45.027 passing through Garsdale with an up coal train on 31 January 1978. Snow and fog is a not unusual mixture in this part of the world.

Bottom left: The return of the sun to Garsdale on 23 March 1979. No 40.100 slows down to allow a linesman to step down from the cab where he had been thawing out his feet from walking the frozen track.

Right: The sun still shone on the following day as No 40.105 passed through Garsdale with the morning Carlisle-Severn Tunnel junction freight. What appears to be a snow filled gully in the left foreground of this picture is in fact the 'coal road' to Dent station.

Below: Garsdale sunset on 30 January 1978. No 45.010 is seen with 8E15 the Carlisle-Healey Mills freight at 16.10.

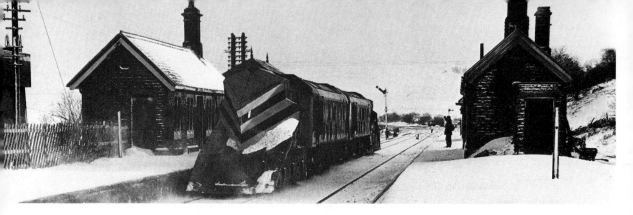

Above: The snow plough unit comprising Nos 25.044 and 25.246 working through Garsdale on 22 March 1979 by which time much of the drifting had already been cleared by normal working.

Centre left & bottom left: On the sadly rare occasions when steam specials are allowed on the Settle-Carlisle line Garsdale is used as a watering point. Here we see two of the prime examples of the work of Sir Nigel Gresley working in opposite directions over the line. The earlier shot shows Class A3 4-6-2 No 4472 *Flying Scotsman* on a up special on 16 June 1978. The second picture views the down working of the 'Aire-Eden Limited' hauled by Class A4 4-6-2 No 4498 *Sir Nigel Gresley* on 21 October 1978.

Above: Some slight reminder of the days of yore is seen when the stations involved in Dales Rail services come to life. Here Gloucester RCW Co Driver Trailer Composite (Class 143) No E56303 is paired with Metro-Cammell Motor Brake Second (Class 101/2) No E50217 to form the up Dales Rail working seen at Garsdale at 19.07 on 20 August 1978.

Centre left: Another link with the past is the occasional piloting of heavy freights as far as Garsdale. No 25.206 assists No 45.044 on 1 June 1979. The Class 25 later returned light engine.

Bottom left: When all is said and done the only real link between past and present is man, for without him all records and relics are valueless. This scene of the snow bound Garsdale cottages provides a direct link with railway constructors and workers over more than a century.

Garsdale to Ais Gill Viaduct

Garsdale has in its life been variously called Hawes Junction, Hawes Junction and Garsdale, and Garsdale for Hawes. It was of course the point at which the Hawes branch diverged from the main line. As previously noted, the branch was opened in 1878, and closed in 1959 but the alignment and some of its major engineering features can still be seen by travellers on the A684 between the Moorcock Inn and Hawes village. In the halcyon steam days of yore pilot engines were detached here and turned on the stockaded turntable for the return to Hellifield or Carlisle and even today an occasional heavy freight is double-headed to this point.

The main line also follows a road, the B6259 which runs from the Moorcock Inn to Kirkby Stephen and although it therefore traverses a relatively inhabited area passing both the aforementioned Moorcock Inn and the Garsdale, Moorcock and Ais Gill railway cottages together with various farm buildings at Lunds Fell and Shaw Paddock, it can be one of the most desolate and uninviting sections of the whole line. I have known Lunds Fell to be bitterly cold and misty when sunshine could be found within 3 or 4 miles in virtually any direction one chose to travel. The Moorcock/Garsdale area sees the confluence of the valleys of the Eden, Ure and Clough and within this area, on Baugh Fell, rises a fourth major river, the Lune. The area is totally dominated by Peaks rising to over 2,000ft (610m) and the line itself is always above 1,100ft (335m). In steam days the 1 in 165 climb away from the Moorcock towards Shotlock tunnel formed a final hurdle for locomotives after what had been a comparatively easy 7 miles (11.3km) from the minor summit in Blea Moor tunnel; this relatively level stretch being possible because of the smoothing and straightening of the valleys by glacial action. Unfortunately this easing of the railway builder's task had associated drawbacks in that the glacial deposit overlaying the bed-rock was often totally unsuitable for the foundations of viaducts or the construction of stable embankments. It was such a deposit, at Dandry Mire, which forced the construction of a viaduct rather that the originally planned embankment and difficulties were also experienced in embankment stabilisation north of Ais Gill box.

Leaving Hawes junction the line swings north through almost 90 degrees, crosses Dandry Mire viaduct and heads for the Eden Valley, cutting through further glacial drifts at Moorcock tunnel, and crossing a small viaduct at Lunds just beyond which, north of Grisedale crossing, was the scene of a 'famous' disaster in 1910. After a further short tunnel through the glacial drift at Shotlock we reach the summit of 1,169ft (356m) at Ais Gill box.

Immediately after emerging from Moorcock tunnel the northern skyline is broken by the Millstone Grit capped flat top of Wild Boar

Fell at 2,324ft (708m) and increasingly this peak and the eastern side of the Mallerstang Valley, Mallerstang Edge, with its peak of High Seat some 2,328ft (710m) loom over both rail borne and road traveller.

Shortly after passing Ais Gill box, Hell Gill Beck, the primary source of the Eden, can be seen leaping off a rocky shelf on the right of the line. Then once again the unique nature of the Settle-Carlisle line shows itself in that, scorning the relatively lush, easy, countryside into which the Eden flows, the route follows the flank of Wild Boar Fell; remaining at an 'altitude' of 1,100ft (335m) and immediately, as in Dent Dale, the railway begins to dominate and stand out from, the landscape rather than merging with it, as does the road to Kirkby Stephen which follows more closely the meandering Eden 200ft (61m) below. The reason for this apparently odd behaviour can be seen if the problem is approached from the other direction, for here is a similar situation to that at Ribblehead where, in order to restrict the ruling gradient to 1 in 100 the relatively easy course of the river valley floor must be ignored. This section is terminated at Ais Gill Beck where the cutting back of the valley side by the post glacial stream forced the contractors into the construction of a beautiful four arch viaduct some 75ft high. This is a smaller but equivalent feature to the much more spectacular Arten Gill viaduct in Dent Dale but unlike that structure it is seen at its best from above the rocky gorge of the Gill rather than from the valley road.

Despite the deceptively flat area between the peaks, this is still mountain country with all the vagaries of weather and terrain which that implies. There can be beautiful mild days, even in winter and long periods of warm summer weather have been known (so I am told) but always there is the threat of wind and rain which find their way inside the heaviest clothes or mist in which all sense of direction is lost. Winter adds impassable snowdrifts with footprints, ruts and other edges frozen to razor sharpness capable of shredding the toe caps. Only the hardy descendants of the Norse sheep farmers, pursuing still their trade, can harbour warm thoughts of this desolate land.

Below: **Both tracks have been completely covered by snow in this shot of No 40.109 with the Healey Mills-Carlisle freight passing through Garsdale at 18.07 on 21 March 1979.**

Above: Hawes station at the end of the branch from Garsdale is undergoing some restoration as an information centre although this June 1979 photograph shows a desolate and overgrown scene.

Below: No 4472 *Flying Scotsman* storms away from Garsdale across Dandrymire with the 'Lord Bishop' memorial tour for Bishop Eric Treacy on 30 September 1978.

Top right: An August afternoon in 1978 finds the photographer basking in the sunshine beside the chapel on the Sedburgh road as No 47.377 crosses Dandrymire viaduct with a down freight.

Right: On 25 August 1978 No 40.086 is seen crossing Dandrymire viaduct with the 16.05 Nottingham-Carlisle. The chapel referred to in the previous photograph is the small building in the centre foreground. The Hawes branch alignment can be seen emerging from behind the bushes beyond the fifth coach and diverging from the Settle-Carlisle line to the left of the picture.

Above left: After crossing Dandrymire the line passes over the Hawes-Sedburgh road and enters Moorcock tunnel. No 40.109 is seen with a down coal train just after crossing the road bridge. The Hawes branch alignment can be clearly seen in the background.

Left: The lush grasses of August had disappeared, covered by the snow of March 1979 as a Class 40 hauled up van train approached Dandrymire on 22 March 1979.

Above: A typically dramatic Settle-Carlisle sky silhouettes a Class 40 hauled cement train crossing the road bridge over the Hawes-Sedburgh road. The Garsdale cottages can be seen on the right of the picture.

Below: No 40.046 with a Carlisle-Healey Mills freight approaches the northern portal of Moorcock tunnel from Lunds Fell on 1 June 1979.

Above: The bleakness of the countryside between Garsdale and Ais Gill can be clearly seen in this July 1977, shot of No 40.076 crossing Lunds viaduct. Such trees as are visible are small and stunted and thin out rapidly as one leaves the sheltered hollows. The main group of trees in the foreground are growing in the quarry from which the stone was obtained to build Lunds viaduct. The white painted cottages in the mid-distance were still British Rail property in 1979 and designated numbers 1 and 2 Grisedale Crossing Cottages. The switchback road from the Moorcock Inn to Kirkby Stephen can be seen to the right of the railway line.

Below: The same scene from slightly west of the previous view sees Class 47 hauled 09.35 Carlisle-Nottingham traversing a bleak winter landscape on 22 March 1979. The pure white snow of Wild Boar Fell dominates the distant horizon. At this time the Kirkby Stephen road was barely passable, and the village of Outh Gill had only recently returned to civilisation after being cut off for several days. The railway continued to operate throughout the winter. Notwithstanding the rigors of life in the area and the arduous work for a linesman on the Settle-Carlisle, anyone fortunate enough to live in Grisedale Crossing cottages was assured of a grandstand view as a succession of locomotives roared out of Moorcock tunnel and across Lunds viaduct.

Above: A photographer's dream as No 40.097 on a down freight emerges from Moorcock tunnel and meets No 40.094 with an up working. Having had luck of this kind the photographer can only hope for a similar situation on a better day or 'resort' to the type of picture shown on the following pages.

Below: BR Class 9F 2-10-0 No 92220 *Evening Star* crosses Lunds viaduct on 13 May 1978. It was whilst waiting at Appleby to photograph this train that the The Rev Eric Treacy former Bishop of Wakefield collapsed and died.

Above: Steam first returned to the Settle-Carlisle line on 25 March 1978 with the running of the 'Norfolkman' hauled by No 4771 seen here storming towards Grisedale Crossing. This train was named the 'Norfolkman' as a tribute to Mr D. W. (Bill) Harvey sometime shedmaster of Norwich under whose direction the engine had been restored.

Top right: Whatever may have been the advantage of the Midland Railway's provision of living accommodation in 1875 there can be no doubt that many of the railway cottages rapidly lost the label of desirable residences as the 20th century

progressed. Here we see the interior of one of the Grisedale Crossing cottages in October 1978.

Right: No 47.361 approaches Grisedale Crossing with the Carlisle-Healey Mills afternoon freight on 29 May 1979. The train has just passed the point at which the infamous derailment of 24 December 1910 occurred when the midnight express from St Pancras to Glasgow struck two light engines returning from Hawes junction to Carlisle. Of the 12 victims of the accident three were never identified and their remains are buried in Hawes church yard.

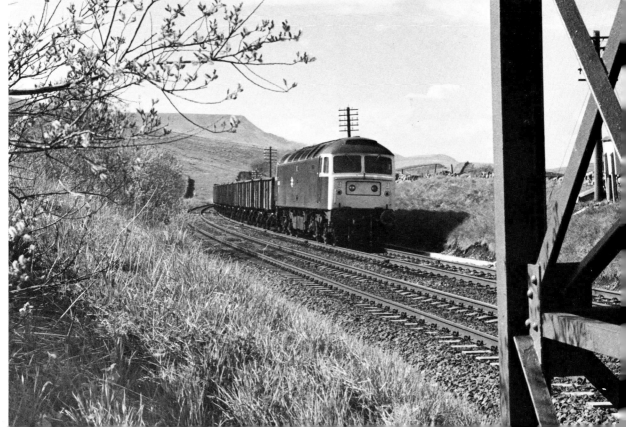

Above: Grisedale Crossing, Lunds viaduct and Moorcock tunnel seen from slightly south of the point of the 1910 derailment as No 45.077 hurries the 09.35 Carlisle-Nottingham through a lull in the blizzard of 31 January 1978.

Below: Mist rises from Wild Boar Fell as No 40.197 crosses Lunds at 07.55 on 1 June 1979.

Top right: No 25.105 and 25.149 are seen crossing Lunds Fell with 6S82 Pennyford-Gunnie at 16.50 on 8 May 1978.

Below right: Checking the track gauge south of Shotlock tunnel on 3 June 1979.

Above left & left: A winter and summer view from above the southern portal of Shotlock tunnel. 15 June 1978 sees No 4472 on a down private special comprising the McAlpine saloons. Earlier in the year on 30 January 1978, No 47.013 approaches the same position with a Clitheroe-Hexham freight.

Above: On the same day as the previous photograph, No 40.156 is seen approaching the northern portal of Shotlock tunnel with the afternoon Carlisle-Healey Mills goods.

Right: Snow covered Wild Boar Fell is seen in the background as No 40.144 approaches the northern portal of Shotlock tunnel in January 1978. At this point the Moorcock-Kirkby Stephen road comes close the line and can be seen on the right of the picture.

Above: A more typically Settle-Carlisle wet day in October 1978, sees No 4498 blasting out of the northern portal of Shotlock with a down special to Carlisle.

Below: The lonely outpost of Ais Gill signalbox has inspired endless romantic prose on the Settle-Carlisle line. The reality is less romantic as this 31 January 1978 photograph shows.

Above right: No 40.125 passes Ais Gill box with an up freight in August 1978.

Right: Signalman's view towards Wild Boar Fell 1974.
Peter R. Walton

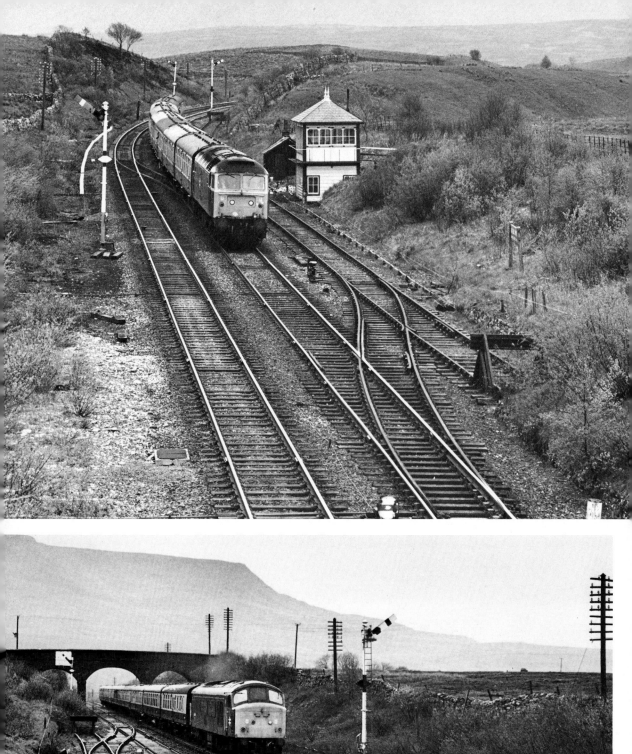

Left: No 47.459 brings the 09.40 Leicester-Glasgow past Ais Gill box on 2 June 1979. Note the summit board on the right. The road over Shotlock hill can be seen in the extreme right background.

Below left: Any day can be a wet and miserable day as this May 1979 picture taken at Ais Gill summit shows. The 11.50 Glasgow-Nottingham is seen approaching Ais Gill signalbox with the summit sign on the left. The bridge under which the train is passing is a double bridge which in addition to giving access to the limestone gorge of Hell Gill Beck, the major headwater of the Eden, marks the crossing point of a major green track along which the famous Lady Anne Clifford journeyed between her castles in the Eden Valley and Yorkshire.

Above: Ais Gill Moor casts its shadow closer and closer to the line as No 25.246 starts on the long down grade from Ais Gill with a mixed goods in the early afternoon of 30 January 1978.

Below: No 45.013 just north of Ais Gill summit with the 07.15 Nottingham-Glasgow on 30 January 1978.

Above & left: The traditional viewpoint for photographing southbound trains approaching Ais Gill summit is just south of the road bridge from which the previous shot was taken with Wild Board Fell in the background. The winter photograph shows No 45.020 with the 11.50 Glasgow-Nottingham approaching Ais Gill early in a January afternoon in 1978, whilst the summer photograph shows No 45.141 with the 16.10 Glasgow-Nottingham on a June evening in 1979. In addition to showing wildly contrasting weather conditions the two photographs are of interest in relation to the relative sun positions in summer and winter.

Top right: Between 1962 and 1963 Class A3 Pacifics allocated to Leeds Holbeck worked the principal expresses. This picture taken on 1 September 1963, by which time many expresses were Type 4 diesel hauled, shows No 60038 *Firdaussi* silhouetted against Wild Boar Fell, in splendid isolation, with the relief to the up 'Thames-Clyde Express', making easy work of the last few hundred yards of the climb to Ais Gill. *G. W. Morrison*

Centre right: Unfortunately whenever steam appears now-a-days the splendid wilderness is transformed into something of a fair ground as can be seen in this 16 June 1978 shot of No 4472 *Flying Scotsman* approaching Ais Gill.

Bottom right: Relative isolation once more and No 40.049 is seen south of the road bridge at Ais Gill with the 16.05 Nottingham-Carlisle. From this point, the Kirkby Stephen road follows roughly the line of the river whilst the railway clings to the side of the Mallerstang Valley.

Left: The conventional view of Ais Gill viaduct from the southern side of the beck sees No 47.043 with the 15.15 Glasgow-Nottingham on a sunny Sunday in May 1979.

Below left: No 47.053 with the 16.10 Glasgow-Nottingham on 29 May 1979, crossing Ais Gill viaduct. The wooden bridge under which the train has just passed is called Hangman's Bridge and is said to be thus named because a platelayer committed suicide by attaching a rope to the bridge and leaping over the edge.

Above: Move up the flank of Wild Boar Fell on the southern side of Ais Gill Beck and the 75ft high viaduct rapidly blends into the scenery as does this unidentified Class 47 with an up goods on 1 June 1979.

Below: From the Moorcock-Kirkby Stephen road, Ais Gill viaduct appears relatively insignificant except at its immediate foot. No 4472 *Flying Scotsman* is seen with an up special in June 1978, climbing towards Ais Gill.

Ais Gill Viaduct to Appleby

This section sees a complete transition from the grandiose grey/green limestone country, where the main feature of the scenery is the interplay of the light and shade of the cloud shadows on the hillsides, to the verdant pastures and forests overlying the red sandstone of the Eden Valley, where much of the countryside is the typically 'English' landscape of village, field and hedgerow.

From Ais Gill the line makes use of the Eden Valley for a short distance but in order to keep the gradient to manageable proportions it askews the valley floor and, after cutting into the hills passes west of Kirkby Stephen using subsidiary streams and in particular the Helm Beck. Following the valley nearer to Warcop and thence to Kirkby Stephen would have added considerably to the gradient from Kirkby Stephen to Ais Gill and so important was the concept of the Settle-Carlisle as a main line to Scotland that the major market town of Kirkby Stephen was thereby by-passed, served only by Kirkby Stephen West station, which lies some $1\frac{1}{4}$ miles from the centre of the town.

After crossing Ais Gill viaduct the line clings to the side of Wild Boar Fell with the Eden far below, to Birkett tunnel, where a geological fault presented the engineers with a veritable 'hotch potch' of limestone grit, coal, iron, magnesium limestone and shale. Some idea of the problems which must have been encountered can still be ascertained by an inspection of the rocks in the cutting approaching the southern portal. Birkett to Kirkby Stephen West makes use of the western extremity of the Eden Valley but from then on the line strikes boldly north west and the river is lost to sight. The fact that the line is now, as it were, crossing the grain of the countryside rather than following a major river valley means that a succession of earthworks and engineering features is required and many of these are relatively inaccessible to the photographer or student of railway construction when compared with those of the more open glacial valleys. The traveller going north on the railway is presented with a succession of cuttings, embankments, bridges, and one major tunnel, Helm, at bewildering speed and the only obvious change in the countryside is a gradual increase in the number of trees. Then suddenly, once Ormside viaduct is crossed, the limestone country is at an end and all is red and gold and we rest at Appleby; former County Town of Westmoreland. Before local government reorganisation in 1974 Appleby laid claim to being England's smallest county town with a history traceable to before the Norman conquest and having a corporation dating to 1201. Appleby station was unusual in being built of brick but shows its family relationship to the other stations of the line in being unmistakably Derby Gothic. Although the town lies within a huge loop of the Eden, the railway does not 'lower itself' to the extent of crossing the river and entering the older part of the town but stands over 100ft above the river facing the Norman castle, which holds the high ground within the river meander.

The Eden is born in the Millstone Grit, passes through grey limestone country to reach the pink Brockram, half and half, town of Kirkby Stephen but begins to mature and lose its thrusting, youthful, vigour in the soft New Red Sandstone town of Appleby. Thus it is with the railway.

Below: No 4498 *Sir Nigel Gresley* makes a spirited climb along the side of the Mallerstang Valley on 22 October 1978. This view is taken from the Kirkby Stephen load looking across the river towards the western side of the valley.

Above left: After waiting in sunshine for some hours the author's enthusiasm was dented by what is no doubt technically correctly but euphemistically referred to as 'heavy precipitation' on 13 May 1978. Nevertheless *Evening Star* was able to lighten somewhat an otherwise dull landscape just south of Birkett tunnel in charge of the 'Border Venturer' which was steam hauled to Leeds where it was due at 19.54.

Left: The embankment in the previous photograph is followed immediately by the deep cutting approach to Birkett tunnel. No 45.010 approaches the cutting with the 10.20 Nottingham-Glasgow on 13 May 1978.

Above: Casual visitors to the Settle-Carlisle often comment on the substantial structure of apparently minor bridges. It should be remembered however that at the time of the railway's original construction in 1875 what today appear as minor farm roads were established lines of communication of some consequence. This bridge which guards the approach to the cutting south of Birkett tunnel is a beautiful structure by any standard. No 47.433 is seen with the 11.50 Glasgow-Nottingham on the afternoon of 9 May 1978. The cutting at the approach to Birkett tunnel can be seen through the arch of the bridge.

Right: British Railways Standard Pacific No 70025 *Western Star* storms away from the southern port of Birkett tunnel with an up freight in March 1967. *L. A. Nixon*

Above: With the river now some several hundred feet below, the line enters Birkett tunnel. A Class 25 hauled up freight is seen in the cutting approaching the bridge shown on page 81.

Below: Linesmen stand aside to allow No 45.024 with the 07.15 Nottingham-Glasgow to leave the northern portal of Birkett tunnel on a dull morning in May 1978.

Above right: Powerless No 84.009 is ignominiously escorted towards the northern portal of Birkett tunnel by No 40.139 on the morning of 23 August 1978.

Right: Bulleid Pacific No 35028 *Clan Line* leaves a white plume across the eastern edge of the upper Eden Valley as it approaches Birkett tunnel with the return leg of the 'Lord Bishop' special on 30 September 1978. *G. W. Morrison*

Left: No 40.070 with the 09.35 Carlisle-Nottingham is seen south of Kirkby Stephen West at Bull Gill. The road at this point is often guarded by two particularly unfriendly sheep dogs the length of whose tethers allows the pedestrian access only by plotting a careful course up the centre of the track.

Below: Taking it easy whilst exchanging views on locomotive performance over the Long Drag, we see the crews of a double-headed down freight led by Stanier Class 8F No 48268 which was being held temporarily at Kirkby Stephen because of a minor derailment at Appleby on a day in April 1967. *L. A. Nixon*

Bottom: Local services over the line were withdrawn from 5 May 1970. That day was still four years in the future when this shot was taken of an up local leaving Kirkby Stephen. The typical trailing junction used at all Settle-Carlisle stations together with the crossover to the goods shed can be clearly seen. *L. A. Nixon*

Right: Class 5 4-6-0 No 44675 roars through Kirkby Stephen West with an up freight in April 1967. The load consisted of 44 wagons and a brake van. *L. A. Nixon*

Below right: Full effort from British Railways Standard Pacific No 70024 *Vulcan* as she blasts out of the cutting north of Kirkby Stephen with an up freight in April 1967. *L. A. Nixon*

Top: With considerably less fuss and effort but consequently less glamour and excitement No 47.197 approaches Kirkby Stephen West with the 09.35 Carlisle-Nottingham on a dull day in October 1978. Note that telegraph wires seen in the previous picture have been buried and the poles removed.

Above: No 25.103 with down empty carriage stock through Kirkby Stephen West on 23 October 1978. It may be noted that the station buildings are little changed from the 1967 shot seen earlier.

Left: Unless diversions are in progress, Sundays see little activity except for engineering maintenance work. Unfortunately for the maintenance gangs the Settle-Carlisle line is a prime example of the saying that it always rains on Sundays and 21 August 1978, was no exception as No 25.191 was ballasting south of Smardale viaduct.

Above right & right: No 4472 *Flying Scotsman* is seen with special 1Z12 'The Moorlands', which had gone north via Shap, climbing south towards Kirkby Stephen West on 26 October 1968. At this time *Flying Scotsman* was the only steam locomotive allowed on British Rail track.

Above: Slightly north of the previous view No 40.026 is seen with a down freight in May 1978.

Top right: No 25.200 near Waitby south of Smardale viaduct with an up freight in May 1978.

Right: Stanier 'Black Five' 4-6-0 No 45373 obliterates the view of Smardale viaduct with her effort on an up freight in early 1967. *L. A. Nixon*

Left: No 40.080 crosses Crosby Garrett viaduct with the 11.50 Glasgow-Nottingham on a cloudy 21 August 1978. The viaduct is 55ft high and 110yd long, the stone for its construction having been taken from the adjacent cutting.

Below left: Seen from the fellside, Crosby Garrett viaduct seems to blend with the village but totally dominates the tiny hamlet when viewed from the street. A '9F' hauled Long Meg-Widnes anhydrite train is seen crossing the viaduct in 1967. *L. A. Nixon*

Above: No 4771 *Green Arrow* south of Helm tunnel at Breaks Hall with the return leg of the Easter 1978 specials.

Below: Double-headed Class 5 4-6-0 Nos 44871 and 44781 on the famous, or infamous, British Railway 15gn 'End of Steam' special are seen heading south towards Crosby Garrett on 11 August 1968. *L. A. Nixon*

Top left: Class 9F 2-10-0 No 92223 drifts towards Appleby with the Widnes-Long Meg anhydrite empties on 30 April 1967. *L. A. Nixon*

Left: Eleven years later Bulleid Pacific No 35028 *Clan Line* is seen leaving Appleby with the 'Lord Bishop' special on 30 September 1978. *L. A. Nixon*

Above: Stanier 'Black Five' No 45295 is seen running into Appleby from the south with a down pick up freight in August 1966. *L. A. Nixon*

Right: Pick-up freights are long gone but passenger trains pick-up a fair number of humans even on weekdays as this shot of a Monday afternoon up train in September 1979, shows.

Appleby to Carlisle

From Appleby to Carlisle the line traverses the Vale of Eden, some 30 miles of verdant pasture and forest punctuated by the glow of the New Red Sandstone whether used as building material or uncovered by the construction of the railway. The Eden is a mature river valley and except for the section between Lazonby and Armathwaite is broader and flatter than much of the Ribble. Nevertheless the railway makes much the same use of this valley as it did of the valley of the southern river eschewing the temptation to follow the easy contours close to the stream in the interests of maintaining its main line status. The necessity to maintain both the alignment and gradient of a main line often finds it some 50 to 100ft (15 to 30m) above the river level. This incidentally keeps the line less subject to flooding as well as allowing it to pass through a number of hamlets which have developed from settlements made on the bluff above the river. The height gained between Carlisle and Appleby had to be such that the limiting ruling gradient of 1 in 100 could be maintained southwards from Appleby.

A number of interesting rivers are tributary to the Eden over this section, in particular the Eamont which flows from Ullswater and the Lyvennet which rises on Crosby Ravensworth Fell and whose waters refreshed the army of Charles II one evening in 1651. The total impression of fertile, well kept, farmland throughout the whole of the Eden Valley is in total contrast to the virtual siege economy, hill farms, of the more southern sections. Although many factors combine to underline the differences between the cruel mountain sections and this relatively mild and welcoming area, the most noticeable to the casual visitor is rainfall. The rainfall in the valley north of Appleby is something of the order of 35in per year compared with double that in the hills with a record of $109\frac{1}{2}$in having been recorded at Ribblehead in 1954.

From an engineering point of view this section is surprisingly interesting, particularly in the area of the Eden Gorge between Lazonby and Armathwaite but because it lacks the romance of the hill sections, is somewhat less accessible, hemmed in by private land and mellowed by the signs of cultivation; it has not attracted the photographic following of the more spectacular mountain section with its open views of structures such as Ribblehead, Dent Head, and Arten Gill viaducts. Whilst keeping some 100ft (30.5m) above the river level, the line broadly follows the gradient of the valley but makes a number of climbs to minor summits in traversing the broken ground away from the river valley floor. As has been said before, this is in keeping with the necessity to make height by Appleby in order to limit the gradient between Appleby and Ais Gill but in so doing the engineering works of the line become much more interesting than would have a series of low level bridges built to cross the river meanders. The manner in which the line follows the side of the gorge between Lazonby and Armathwaite is somewhat reminiscent of the alignment of the WCML in the Lune Gorge below Tebay.

Before the spate of closures on 5 May 1970, there were some 10 stations on this stretch in addition to Appleby and Carlisle, all conforming to the Midland image but built in local stone and to this extent blending with the landscape. Many of these station buildings survive, often in use for storage of railway maintenance materials but officially closed, although Langwathby, Lazonby, and Armathwaite are a part of the Dales Rail scheme and Armathwaite has been used on occasions by steam specials.

The Vale of Eden can be a place of breathtaking beauty. There can be few finer sights than that offered to the traveller fortunate enough to look down into the Gorge on a sunny Autumn morning as the mist rises from the river, wrapping forest and railway in Transylvanian mystery. Were it not diminished by being the northern section of the Settle-Carlisle line it would be a place which drew photographers from far and wide. Unfortunately its gentle beauty must, always and ever, be overshadowed by the savage splendour of the southern sections.

The Settle-Carlisle railway actually enters Carlisle on the track of the former North Eastern Railway which it joins at Petteril Bridge junction. Just south of this junction, at Durran Hill, was the original engine shed for the northern section. This shed was closed in 1936 and its duties transferred to Carlisle Kingmoor. The sidings at this location were closed in 1962. The original Carlisle Kingmoor shed is now closed and the various steam age features totally removed. Prior to being taken over by electrification, which always tends to give stations a somewhat claustrophobic air, Carlisle Citadel was a splendid station and still retains a little of its former atmosphere, grown out of over a century of joint useage by many railway companies. Nevertheless arrival at Carlisle is always something of an anticlimax after the splendours of the journey, for if ever it were true to say that to travel hopefully is better than to arrive, it was true of the Settle-Carlisle railway. Long may it remain so.

Below: A Class 40 has backed its train into the branch at Penrith junction to allow the passage of the (late) 11.50 Glasgow-Nottingham hauled by No 45.055 on 24 September 1979. The junction gave access to the NE lines to Penrith and Kirkby Stephen. The southern section of this line, the Eden Valley branch, is still used to serve the Warcop Army Ranges.

Above: No 40.166 passing under the beautiful footbridge at Appleby station in September 1979. This train had been seen earlier approaching Lazonby (see page 102).

Left: The 08.00 St Pancras-Glasgow departing Appleby hauled by No 45.073 on 3 April 1976. Through daytime working from London to Glasgow ceased with the introduction of the May 1976 timetable.

Top right: No 40.070 at Hale Grange between Long Marton and New Biggin with the 07.15 Nottingham-Glasgow on 27 March 1978.

Right: Ex-LNER Class V2 2-6-2 No 4771 *Green Arrow* south of Newbiggin with an up special on 27 March 1978.

Top left: No 40.030 approaches Culgaith level crossing with a down cement train in October 1978.

Left: Culgaith crossing and signalbox with the remains of the station beyond on 23 October 1978, is passed by an up freight hauled by No 25.103. The southern portal of Culgaith tunnel, from above which the following shot was taken, can be seen in the left background.

Above: BR Class 9F 2-10-0 No 92220 *Evening Star* drifts towards Culgaith tunnel with a down special on 30 September 1978.   *L. A. Nixon*

Right: No 47.150 passes the confluence of the Rivers Eamont and Eden with a Hunslet-Carlisle freight on 11 May 1978.

Left & below: Ex-LNER Class A4 4-6-2
No 4498 *Sir Nigel Gresley* south of
Langwathby with an up special on
22 October 1978. This is an arable farming
area in total contrast to the upland grazing
areas of the southern section.

Right: BR Class 9F 2-10-0 No 92220
Evening Star at Langwathby with the
'Border Venturer' special on 13 May 1978.
L. A. Nixon

Below right: In pouring northern rain
No 47.202 takes the 11.50 Glasgow-
Nottingham through Little Salkeld on
11 May 1978.

Above left: No 40.047 passes Long Meg sidings with the 11.50 Glasgow-Nottingham on 23 October 1978. These sidings were the origin for the '9F' hauled anhydrite trains which feature in many of the 1967 shots in this volume.

Left: No 40.166 approaches Lazonby with an up freight in September 1979. Lazonby tunnel can be seen in the right background. The scene is typical of much of this section other than the Eden Gorge.

Above: The morning mist has not fully cleared from the forest clothing the western side of the Eden gorge as No 40.126 rolls a heavy mixed freight towards Baron Wood No 2 tunnel at 09.35 on 24 September 1979.

Right: A Class 40 hauled up freight leaves the southern portal of Armathwaite tunnel high above the Eden Gorge on 24 September 1979.

Left: A Class 47 leaves the northern portal of Armathwaite tunnel with a down freight on 24 September 1979.

Below: No 40.014 between Armathwaite tunnel and the viaduct in September 1979.

Right: No 46.025 at Armathwaite station with the 10.25 Nottingham-Glasgow in August 1979. The goods shed on the left was closed in 1964.

Below right: No 40.107 with the 07.15 Nottingham-Glasgow at Duncowfold two miles south of Cumwhinton. The hills in the background rise to 780ft (238m) with the Pennines beyond rising to over 1,900ft (590m) between the Vale of Eden and the now abandoned NER Haltwhistle-Alston branch line.

Top left: In the autumn of 1967 ex-Great Western 'Castle' class 4-6-0 No 7029 *Clun Castle* visited Eastern and Midland Regions to work a series of excursions. On Saturday 30 September *Clun Castle* worked an A4 Locomotive Society special from Peterborough to Carlisle and was booked to work the return on Sunday 1 October. The 'Castle' is seen making good progress as she approaches Cumwhinton sidings but later had to be removed at Leeds because of large quantities of cotton waste in the water. *L. A. Nixon*

Centre left: On 21 August 1979, No 47.210 with the 11.50 Glasgow-Nottingham passes the site of the former Midland Railway shed at Durran Hill, having just diverged from the ex-North Eastern line to Newcastle. The Newcastle line can be seen in the background paralleling the Settle line.

Bottom left: Carlisle Citadel was constructed jointly by the Lancaster & Carlisle (destined to become part of the London & North Western) and the Caledonian Railway Companies to a 'Gothic' design by William Tate. It was opened on 1 September 1847, with a single platform but various acts extended both platforms and the composition of the Management Committee so that eventually at the time of the Grouping in 1923 no less than six companies made use of its facilities; LNWR, Caledonian Railway, Glasgow & South Western, Midland Railway, North British and North Eastern. This 1966 shot shows the north end from beyond the road over-bridge with an LMS 'Jinty' Class 3F 0-6-0T No 47326 awaiting duty as an English Electric Type 4 (now Class 40) brings in a down passenger train. *L. A. Nixon*

Top right: Ten years later on 3 April 1976, No 45.073 backs on to a Dumfries and Kilmarnock line train, after leaving the, by then unnamed 'Thames-Clyde', 08.00 St Pancras-Glasgow, to be taken on by a Class 86 electric locomotive.

Centre right: No 4498 *Sir Nigel Gresley* being serviced at Carlisle Kingmoor (12A) after working in a special from Leeds over the S&C on 27 August 1967.

Bottom right: BR Standard Pacific No 70038 *Robin Hood* at Carlisle Kingmoor in August 1967.

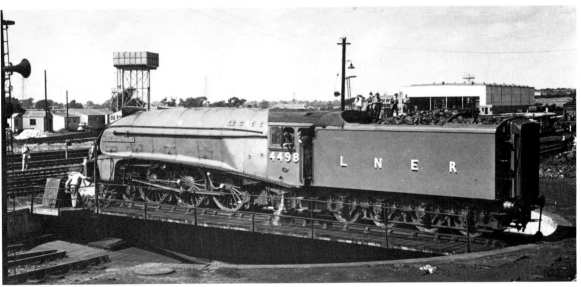

Above: Stanier 'Jubilee' class 4-6-0 No 45593 *Kholapur* on Carlisle Kingmoor (12A) shed in August 1967. This locomotive, together with No 45562 *Alberta* was allocated to Leeds Holbeck (55A) and regularly worked both freight and relief passenger trains over the Settle-Carlisle line during the summer and autumn of 1967.

Below: BR Standard Pacific No 70031 *Byron* at Carlisle Kingmoor in July 1967.

Epilogue

The Penmanshiel tunnel diversions led to the cancellation of the planned steam specials of 1979 but the early months of 1980 saw more steam over the line than at any time since 1967 with the introduction of the 'Cumbrian Mountain Express'. Originally introduced as three northbound and three southbound trains between 19 January and 22 March, the overwhelming demand was such that the total was eventually doubled and the period of operation extended to 19 April. Locomotives were based at Carnforth and the steam route covered Carnforth-Skipton-Carlisle.

Left: 16 February was a particularly miserable day for both passengers and BR with major disruptions due to three separate incidents including the major derailment of the 20.25 Euston-Manchester at Bushey which latter accident resulted in many returning passengers being diverted to Paddington which was reached at 03.15 on Sunday! Most of the mountain journey took place in thick fog and although keeping excellent time over the easy schedule, No 4498 was reported as running 'rough'. With the 'coal road' bridge looming in the background the recalcitrant locomotive is well and truly inspected and discussed by her custodians.

Right: No 5305 leaves Dent on a beautiful and unseasonal 1 March.

Below: No 5305 storms the last mile to Ais Gill between Moorcock and Shotlock tunnels.

Left: Lamplighting time for No 4498 on the 'Cumbrian Mountain Express' at Appleby.

Below: The fog of 16 February has cleared from the 'lowlands' and No 4498 is seen at the Appleby photographic stop.

Bibliography

Mitchell, W. R. & Joy, David; *Settle-Carlisle Railway;* Dalesman Books, 1976

Jenkinson, David; *Rails in the Fells;* Peco Publications, 1973

Baughan, Peter E.; *North of Leeds;* Roundhouse, 1966

Hamilton Ellis, C.; *The Midland Railway;* Ian Allan, 1952

Rolt, L. T. C.; *Red For Danger;* Bodley Head, 1955

Williams, Frederick S.; *The Midland Railway, Its Rise and Progress;* David & Charles, 1968

Raistrick, Dr Arthur; *Old Yorkshire Dales;* David & Charles, 1967

Schneider, Ascanio & Armin, Mase; *Railway Accidents of Great Britain and Europe;* David & Charles, 1968

Jenkinson, David; *Settle-Carlisle Railway: Centenary 1876-1976;* British Rail (LM), 1976

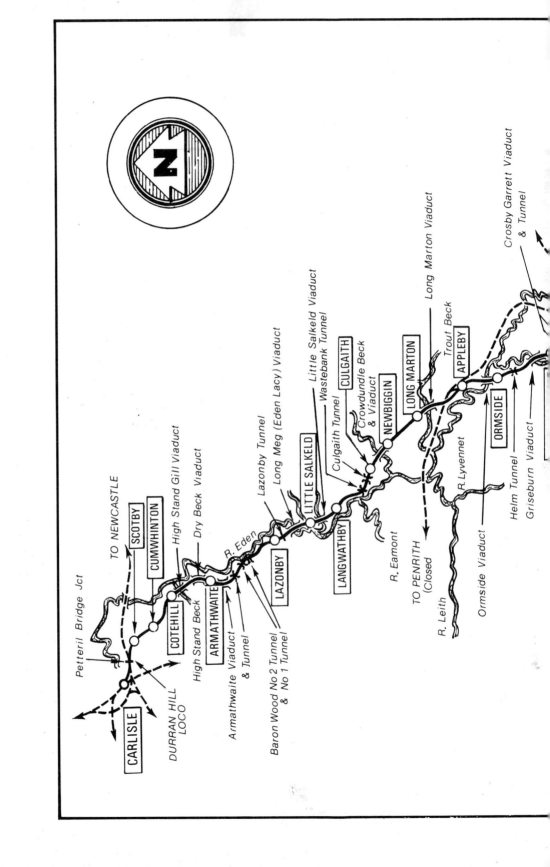